The Selected Poems of
DONALD HALL

POETRY BY DONALD HALL

THE
SELECTED
POEMS OF
DONALD
HALL

Mariner Books
Houghton Mifflin Harcourt
Boston   New York

First Mariner Books edition 2017
Copyright © 2015 by Donald Hall

For information about permission to reproduce selections from
this book, write to trade.permissions@hmhco.com or to Permissions,
Houghton Mifflin Harcourt Publishing Company, 3 Park Avenue,
19th Floor, New York, New York 10016.

hmhco.com

Library of Congress Cataloging-in-Publication Data
Hall, Donald, date.
[Poems. Selections]
The selected poems / of Donald Hall.
pages ; cm
ISBN 978-0-544-55560-0 (hardcover) — ISBN 978-0-544-55561-7 (ebook)
ISBN 978-1-328-74560-6 (pbk.)
I. Title.
PS3515.A3152A6 2015
811'.54 — dc23
2015004341

Book design by Greta D. Sibley

Printed in the United States of America
DOC 10 9 8 7 6 5 4 3 2 1

Andrew Hall
Philippa Smith

CONTENTS

The Selected Poems of
DONALD HALL

My Son My Executioner

My son, my executioner,
   I take you in my arms,
Quiet and small and just astir
   And whom my body warms.

Sweet death, small son, our instrument
   Of immortality,
Your cries and hungers document
   Our bodily decay.

We twenty-five and twenty-two,
   Who seemed to live forever,
Observe enduring life in you
   And start to die together.

The Sleeping Giant

a hill in Connecticut

The whole day long, under the walking sun
That poised an eye on me from its high floor,
Holding my toy beside the clapboard house
I looked for him, the summer I was four.

I was afraid the waking arm would break
From the loose earth and rub against his eyes
A fist of trees, and the whole country tremble
In the exultant labor of his rise;

Then he with giant steps in the small streets
Would stagger, cutting off the sky, to seize
The roofs from house and home because we had
Covered his shape with dirt and planted trees;

And then kneel down and rip with fingernails
A trench to pour the enemy Atlantic
Into our basin, and the water rush,
With the streets full and all the voices frantic.

That was the summer I expected him.
Later the high and watchful sun instead
Walked low behind the house, and school began,
And winter pulled a sheet over his head.

The Lone Ranger

Anarchic badlands spread without a road,
And from the river west no turned-up loam;
No farmer prayed for rain, no settler's horse
But one time blundered riderless to home.

Unfriendly birds would gather in the air,
A circling kind of tombstone. As for the law,
No marshal lived for long unless he could
Defeat his mirror'd image to the draw.

So now he rode upon a silver horse.
He stood for law and order. Anarchy
Like flood or fire roared through every gate
But he and Tonto hid behind a tree

And when the bandits met to split the loot,
He blocked the door. With silver guns he shot
The quick six-shooters from their snatching hands
And took them off to jail and let them rot.

For him the badlands were his mother's face.
He made an order where all order lacked
From Hanged Boy Junction to the Rio Grande.
Why did he wear a mask? He was abstract.

Christmas Eve in Whitneyville

December, and the closing of the year;
The momentary carolers complete
Their Christmas Eves, and quickly disappear
Into their houses on each lighted street.

Each car is put away in each garage;
Each husband home from work, to celebrate,
Has closed his house around him like a cage,
And wedged the tree until the tree stood straight.

Tonight you lie in Whitneyville again,
Near where you lived, and near the woods or farms
Which Eli Whitney settled with the men
Who worked at mass-producing firearms.

The main street, which was nothing after all
Except a school, a stable, and two stores,
Was improvised and individual,
Picking its way alone, among the wars.

Now Whitneyville is like the other places,
Ranch houses stretching flat beyond the square,
Same stores and movie, same composite faces
Speaking the language of the public air.

Old houses of brown shingle still surround
This graveyard where you wept when you were ten
And helped to set a coffin in the ground.
You left a friend from school behind you then,

And now return, a man of fifty-two.
Talk to the boy. Tell him about the years
When Whitneyville quadrupled, and how you
And all his friends went on to make careers,

Had cars as long as hayracks, boarded planes
For Rome or Paris where the pace was slow
And took the time to think how yearly gains,
Profit and volume made the business grow.

"The things I had to miss," you said last week,
"Or thought I had to, take my breath away."
You propped yourself on pillows, where your cheek
Was hollow, stubbled lightly with new gray.

This love is jail; another sets us free.
Tonight the houses and their noise distort
The thin rewards of solidarity.
The houses lean together for support.

The noises fail, and lights go on upstairs.
The men and women are undressing now
To go to sleep. They put their clothes on chairs
To take them up again. I think of how,

All over Whitneyville, when midnight comes,
They lie together and are quieted,
To sleep as children sleep, who suck their thumbs,
Cramped in the narrow rumple of each bed.

They will not have unpleasant thoughts tonight.
They make their houses jails, and they will take
No risk of freedom for the appetite,
Or knowledge of it, when they are awake.

The lights go out and it is Christmas Day.
The stones are white, the grass is black and deep.
I will go back and leave you here to stay
Where the dark houses harden into sleep.

An Airstrip in Essex, 1960

It is a lost road into the air.
It is a desert
among sugar beets.
The tiny wings
of the Spitfires of nineteen forty-one
sink under mud in the Channel.

Near the road a brick pillbox
totters under a load of grass,
where Home Guards waited
in the white fogs of the invasion winter.

Good night, old ruined war.

In Poland the wind rides on a jagged wall.
Smoke rises from the stones; no, it is mist.

The Long River

The musk ox smells
in his long head
my boat coming. When
I feel him there,
intent, heavy,

the oars make wings
in the white night,
and deep woods are close
on either side
where trees darken.

I rowed past towns
in their black sleep
to come here. I passed
the northern grass
and cold mountains.

The musk ox moves
when the boat stops,
in hard thickets. Now
the wood is dark
with old pleasures.

Love Is Like Sounds

Late snow fell this early morning of spring.
At dawn I rose from bed, restless, and looked
Out my window, to wonder if there the snow
Fell outside your bedroom, and you watching.

I played my game of solitaire. The cards
Came out the same the third time through the deck.
The game was stuck. I threw the cards together,
And watched the snow that could not do but fall.

Love is like sounds, whose last reverberations
Hang on the leaves of strange trees, on mountains
As distant as the curving of the earth
Where the snow hangs still in the middle of the air.

White Apples

when my father had been dead a week
I woke
with his voice in my ear
                                    I sat up in bed
and held my breath
and stared at the pale closed door

white apples and the taste of stone

if he called again
I would put on my coat and galoshes

The Alligator Bride

The clock of my day winds down.
The cat eats sparrows outside my window.
Once, she brought me a small rabbit
which we devoured together, under
the Empire table
while the men shrieked
repossessing the gold umbrella.

Now the beard on my clock turns white.
My cat stares into dark corners
missing her gold umbrella.
She is in love
with the Alligator Bride.

Ah, the tiny fine white
teeth! The Bride, propped on her tail
in white lace
stares from the holes
of her eyes. Her stuck-open mouth
laughs at minister and people.

On bare new wood
fourteen tomatoes,
a dozen ears of corn,
six bottles of white wine,
a melon,
a cat,
broccoli,
and the Alligator Bride.

The color of bubble gum,
the consistency of petroleum jelly,
wickedness oozes
from the palm of my left hand.
My cat licks it.
I watch the Alligator Bride.

Big houses like shabby boulders
hold themselves tight
in gelatin.
I am unable to daydream.
The sky is a gun aimed at me.
I pull the trigger.
The skull of my promises
leans in a black closet, gapes
with its good mouth
for a teat to suck.

A bird flies back and forth
in my house that is covered by gelatin
and the cat leaps at it,
missing. Under the Empire table
the Alligator Bride
lies in her bridal shroud.
My left hand
leaks on the Chinese carpet.

"Reclining Figure"

Henry Moore

Then the knee of the wave
turned to stone.

By the cliff of her flank
I anchored,

in the darkness of harbors
laid-by.

The Man in the Dead Machine

High on a slope in New Guinea
the Grumman Hellcat
lodges among bright vines
as thick as arms. In nineteen forty-three,
the clenched hand of a pilot
glided it here
where no one has ever been.

In the cockpit the helmeted
skeleton sits
upright, held
by dry sinews at neck
and shoulder, and by webbing
that straps the pelvic cross
to the cracked
leather of the seat, and the breastbone
to the canvas cover
of the parachute.

Or say that the shrapnel
missed me, I flew
back to the carrier, and every morning
take the train, my pale
hands on a black case, and sit
upright, held
by the firm webbing.

The Repeated Shapes

I have visited men's rooms
in several bars
with the rows
of urinals like old men
and the six-sided odor

of disinfectant.
I have felt the sadness
of the small white tiles,
the repeated shapes
and the unavoidable whiteness.

They are my uncles,
these old men
who are only plumbing,
who throb with tears all night
and doze in the morning.

The Days

Ten years ago this minute, he possibly sat
in the sunlight, in Connecticut, in an old chair;
a car may have stopped in the street outside;
he may have turned his head; his ear may have itched.
Since it was September, he probably saw
single leaves dropping from the maple tree.
If he was reading, he turned back to his book,
and perhaps the smell of roses in a pot
came together with the smell of cheese sandwiches
and the smell of a cigarette
smoked by his father who was not dead then.

The moments of that day dwindled
to the small notations of clocks,
and the day busily became another day,
and another, and today, when his hand moves
from his ear which still itches
to rest on his leg, it is marked with the passage
of ten years. Suddenly he has the idea
that thousands and thousands of his days
lie stacked into the ground
like leaves, or like that pressure of green
which turns into coal in a million years.

Though leaves rot, or leaves burn in the gutter;
though the complications of this morning's breakfast
dissolve in faint shutters of light
at a great distance, he continues to daydream
that the past is a country under the ground
where the days practice their old habits
over and over, as faint and persistent
as cigarette smoke in an airless room.
He wishes he could travel there like a tourist
and photograph the unseizable days
in the sunlight, in Connecticut, in an old chair.

Woolworth's

My whole life has led me here.

Daisies made out of resin,
hairnets and motor oil,
Barbie dolls, green
garden chairs,
and forty-one brands of deodorant.

Three hundred years ago
I was hedging and ditching in Devon.
I lacked freedom of worship,
and freedom to trade molasses
for rum, for slaves, for molasses.

"I will sail to Massachusetts
to build the Kingdom
of Heaven on Earth!"

The side of a hill
swung open.
It was Woolworth's!

I followed this vision to Boston.

Digging

One midnight, after a day when lilies
lift themselves out of the ground while you watch them,
and you come into the house at dark
your fingers grubby with digging, your eyes
vague with the pleasure of digging,

let a wind raised from the South
climb through your bedroom window, lift you in its arms
— you have become as small as a seed —
and carry you out of the house, over the black garden,
spinning and fluttering,

and drop you in cracked ground.
The dirt will be cool, rough to your clasped skin
like a man you have never known.
You will die into the ground
in a dead sleep, surrendered to water.

You will wake suffering
a widening pain in your side, a breach
gapped in your tight ribs
where a green shoot struggles to lift itself upward
through the tomb of your dead flesh

to the sun, to the air of your garden
where you will blossom
in the shape of your own self, thoughtless
with flowers, speaking
to bees, in the language of green and yellow, white and red.

The Poem

It discovers by night
what the day hid from it.
Sometimes it turns itself
into an animal.
In summer it takes long walks
by itself where meadows
fold back from ditches.
Once it stood still
in a quiet row of machines.
Who knows
what it is thinking?

The Snow

Snow is in the oak.
Behind the thick, whitening
air which the wind drives,
the weight of the sun
presses the snow
on the pane of my window.

I remember snows and my walking
through their first fall in cities,
asleep or drunk
with the slow, desperate falling.
The snow blurs in my eyes
with other snows.

Snow is what must
come down, even if it struggles
to stay in the air with the strength
of the wind. Like an old man,
whatever I touch I turn
to the story of death.

Snow is what fills
the oak, and what covers
the grass and the bare garden.
Snow is what reverses
the sidewalk and the lawn
into the substance of whiteness.

So the watcher sleeps himself
back to the baby's eyes.
The tree, the breast, and the floor
are limbs of him, and from
his eyes he extends a skin
which grows over the world.

The baby is what must
have fallen, like snow. He resisted,
the way the old man
struggles inside the airy tent
to keep on breathing.
Birth is the fear of death.

Snow is what melts.
I cannot open the door
to the cycles of water.
The sun has withdrawn itself
and the snow keeps falling,
and something will always be falling.

Self-Portrait as a Bear

Here is a fat animal, a bear
that is partly a dodo.
Ridiculous wings hang at his shoulders
as if they were collarbones
while he plods in the bad brickyards
at the edge of the city, smiling
and eating flowers. He eats them
because he loves them
because they are beautiful
because they love him.
It is eating flowers which makes him so fat.
He carries his huge stomach
over the gutters of damp leaves
in parking lots in October,
but inside that paunch
he knows there are fields of lupine
and meadows of mustard and poppy.
He encloses sunshine.
Winds bend the flowers
in combers across the valley,
birds hang on the stiff wind,
at night there are showers, and the sun
lifts through a haze every morning
of the summer in the stomach.

The Stump

1

Today they cut down the oak.
Strong men climbed with ropes
in the brittle tree.
The exhaust of the gasoline saw
was blue in the branches.

It is February. The oak has been dead a year.
I remember the great sails of its branches
rolling out green, a hundred and twenty feet up,
and acorns thick on the lawn.
Nine cities of squirrels lived in that tree.
Today they ran through the snow
squeaking their lamentation.

Yet I was happy that it was coming down.
"Let it come down!" I kept saying to myself
with a joy that was strange to me.
Though the oak was the shade of old summers,
I loved the guttural saw.

2

By night a nude trunk stands up fifteen feet,
and cords of firewood press
on the twiggy frozen grass of the yard.
A man comes every afternoon for a week
to cut the trunk down to earth.

Bluish stains spread through the wood
and make it harder to cut.
He says they are the nails of a trapper
who dried his pelts on the oak
when badgers dug in my lawn.

At the bottom he hacks for two days,
his knuckles scraping the stiff snow.
His chain saw breaks three teeth.
He cannot make the stump smooth. He leaves
one night after early dark.

3

Roots stiffen under the ground
and the frozen street, coiled around pipes and wires.
The stump is a platform of blond wood
in the gray winter. It is nearly level
with the snow that covers the little garden around it.
It is a door into the underground of old summers,
but if I bend down to it, I am lost
in crags and buttes of a harsh landscape
that continues forever. When snow melts
the wood darkens into the ground;
rain and thawed snow move deeply into the stump,
backwards along the disused tunnels.

4

The edges of the trunk turn black.
In the middle there is a pale overlay,
like a wash of chalk on darkness.
The desert of the winter
has moved inside.
I do not step on it now, I am used to it,
like a rock, or a bush that does not grow.

There is a sailing ship
beached in the cove of a small island
where the warm water is turquoise.
The hulk leans over, full of rain and sand,
and shore flowers grow from it.
Then it is under full sail in the Atlantic,
on a blue day, heading for the island.

She has planted sweet alyssum
in the holes where the wood was rotten.
It grows thick, it bulges
like flowers contending from a tight vase.
Now the stump sinks downward into its roots
with a cargo of rain
and white blossoms that last into October.

Mount Kearsarge

Great blue mountain! Ghost.
I look at you
from the porch of the farmhouse
where I watched you all summer
as a boy. Steep sides, narrow flat
patch on top —
you are clear to me
like the memory of one day.
Blue! Blue!
The top of the mountain floats
in haze.
I will not rock on this porch
when I am old. I turn my back on you,
Kearsarge, I close
my eyes, and you rise inside me,
blue ghost.

To a Waterfowl

Women in hats like the rear ends of pink ducks
applauded you, my poems.
These are the women whose husbands I meet on airplanes,
who close their briefcases and ask, "What are *you* in?"
I look in their eyes, I tell them I am in poetry,

and their eyes fill with anxiety, and with little tears.
"Oh, yeah?" they say, developing an interest in clouds.
"My wife, she likes that sort of thing? Hah-hah?
I guess maybe I'd better watch my grammar, huh?"
I leave them in airports, watching their grammar,

and take a limousine to the Women's Goodness Club
where I drink Harvey's Bristol Cream with their wives,
and eat chicken salad with capers, with little tomato wedges,
and I read them "The Erotic Crocodile," and "Eating You."
Ah, when I have concluded the disbursement of my sonorities,

crooning, "High on thy thigh I cry, Hi!"— and so forth —
they spank their wide hands, they smile like Jell-O,
and they say, "Hah-hah? My goodness, Mr. Hall,
but you certainly do have an imagination, huh?"
"Thank you, indeed," I say; "it brings in the bacon."

But now, my poems, now I have returned to the motel,
returned to *l'éternel retour* of the Holiday Inn,
naked, lying on the bed, watching *Godzilla Sucks Mount Fuji*,
addressing my poems, feeling superior, and drinking bourbon
from a flask disguised to look like a transistor radio.

And what about you? You, laughing? You, in the blue jeans,
laughing at your mother who wears hats, and at your father
who rides airplanes with a briefcase watching his grammar?
Will you ever be old and dumb, like your creepy parents?
Not you, not you, not you, not you, not you, not you.

Wolf Knife

from *The Journals of C. F. Hoyt, USN, 1826–1889*

"In mid-August, in the second year
of my First Polar Expedition, the snows and ice of winter
almost upon us, Kantiuk and I
attempted to dash by sledge
along Crispin Bay, searching again for relics
of the Franklin Expedition. Now a storm blew,
and we turned back, and we struggled slowly
in snow, lest we depart land and venture onto ice
from which a sudden fog and thaw
would abandon us to the Providence
of the sea.

       "Near nightfall
I thought I heard snarling behind us.
Kantiuk told me
that two wolves, lean as the bones
of a wrecked ship,
had followed us the last hour, and snapped their teeth
as if already feasting.
I carried but the one charge
in my rifle, since, approaching the second winter,
we rationed stores.

"As it turned dark,
we could push no farther, and made
camp in a corner
of ice-hummocks,
and the wolves stopped also, growling
just past the limits of vision,
coming closer, until I could hear
the click of their claws on ice. Kantiuk laughed
and remarked that the wolves appeared to be most hungry.
I raised my rifle, prepared to shoot the first
that ventured close, hoping
to frighten the other.

               "Kantiuk struck my rifle
down, and said again
that the wolves were hungry, and laughed.
I feared that my old companion
was mad, here in the storm, among ice-hummocks,
stalked by wolves. Now Kantiuk searched
in his pack, and extricated
two knives — *turnoks,* the Inuit called them —
which by great labor were sharpened, on both sides,
to a sharpness like the edge of a barber's razor,
and approached our dogs
and plunged both knives
into the body of our youngest dog
who had limped all day.

                    "I remember
that I considered turning my rifle on Kantiuk
as he approached, then passed me,
carrying knives red with the gore of our dog —
who had yowled, moaned, and now lay
expiring, surrounded
by curious cousins and uncles,
possibly hungry — and thrust the knives
handle-down in the snow.

                        "Immediately
he left the knives, the vague, gray
shapes of the wolves
turned solid, out of the darkness and the snow,
and set ravenously
to licking blood from the honed steel.
The double edge of the knives
so lacerated the tongues of the starved beasts
that their own blood poured
copiously forth
to replenish the dog's blood, and they ate
more furiously than before, while Kantiuk laughed,
and held his sides
laughing.

"And I laughed also,
perhaps in relief that Providence had delivered us
yet again, or perhaps — under conditions of extremity,
far from Connecticut — finding these creatures
acutely ridiculous, so avid
to swallow their own blood. First one, and then the other
collapsed, dying,
bloodless in the snow black with their own blood,
and Kantiuk retrieved
his *turnoks,* and hacked lean meat
from the thigh of the larger wolf,
which we ate
gratefully, blessing the Creator, for we were hungry."

The Coal Fire

A coal fire burned in a basket grate.
We lay in front of it
while ash collected on the firebrick
like snow.
I looked at you, in the small light
of the coal fire: back
delicate, yet with the form of the skeleton,
cheekbones and chin
carved, mouth full,
and breasts like hills of flowers.

The fire was tight and small and endured
when we added a chunk every hour.
The new piece blazed at first
from the bulky shadow of fire,
turning us bright and dark.
Old coals red at the center
warmed us all night.
If we watched all night
we could not tell when the new
coal flaked into ash.

Gold

Pale gold of the walls, gold
of the centers of daisies, yellow roses
pressing from a clear bowl. All day
we lay on the bed, my hand
stroking the deep
gold of your thighs and your back.
We slept and woke
entering the golden room together,
lay down in it breathing
quickly, then
slowly again,
caressing and dozing, your hand sleepily
touching my hair now.

We made in those days
tiny identical rooms inside our bodies
which the men who uncover our graves
will find in a thousand years,
shining and whole.

On Reaching the Age of Two Hundred

When I awoke on the morning
of my two hundredth birthday,
I expected to be consulted
by supplicants
like the Sibyl at Cumae.
I could tell them something.

Instead, it was the usual thing:
dried grapefruit for breakfast,
Mozart all morning, interrupted
by bees' wings,
and making love with a woman
one hundred and eighty-one years old.

At my birthday party
I blew out two hundred candles
one at a time, taking
naps after each twenty-five.
Then I went to bed, at five-thirty,
on the day of my two hundredth birthday,

and slept and dreamed
of a house no bigger than a flea's house
with two hundred rooms in it,
and in each of the rooms a bed,
and in each of the two hundred beds
me sleeping.

Eating the Pig

Twelve people, most of us strangers, stand in a room
in Ann Arbor, drinking Cribari from jars.
Then two young men, who cooked him,
carry him to the table
on a large square of plywood: his body
striped, like a tiger cat's, from the basting,
his legs long, much longer than a cat's,
and the striped hide as shiny as vinyl.

Now I see his head, as he takes his place
at the center of the table,
his wide pig's head; and he looks like the javelina
that ran in front of the car, in the desert outside Tucson,
and I am drawn to him, my brother the pig,
with his large ears cocked forward,
with his tight snout, with his small ferocious teeth
in a jaw propped open
by an apple. How bizarre, this raw apple clenched
in a cooked face! Then I see his eyes,
his eyes cramped shut, his no-eyes, his eyes like X's
in a comic strip when the character gets knocked out.

This afternoon they read directions
from a book: *The eyeballs must be removed*
or they will burst during roasting. So they hacked them out.
"I nearly fainted," says one young man.
"I never fainted before in my whole life."

Then they gutted the pig and stuffed him,
and roasted him for five hours, basting the long body.

Now we examine him, exclaiming, and we marvel at him —
but no one picks up a knife.

Then a young woman cuts off his head.
It comes off so easily, like a detachable part.
With sudden enthusiasm we dismantle the pig,
we wrench his trotters off, we twist them
at shoulder and hip, and they come off so easily.
Then we cut open his belly and pull the skin back.

For myself, I scoop a portion of left thigh,
moist, tender, falling apart, fat, sweet.
We forage like an army starving in winter
that crosses a pass in the hills and discovers
a valley of full barns —
cattle fat and lowing in their stalls,
bins of potatoes in root cellars under white farmhouses,
barrels of cider, onions, hens squawking over eggs —
and the people nowhere, with bread still warm in the oven.

Maybe, south of the valley, refugees pull their carts
listening for Stukas or elephants, carrying
bedding, pans, and silk dresses,
old men and women, children, deserters, young wives.

No, we are here, eating the pig together.

In ten minutes, the destruction is total.

His tiny ribs, delicate as birds' feet, lie crisscrossed.
Or they are like crosshatching in a drawing,
lines doubling and redoubling on each other.

Bits of fat and muscle
mix with stuffing alien to the body,
walnuts and plums. His skin, like a parchment bag
soaked in oil, is pulled back and flattened,
with ridges and humps remaining, like a contour map,
like the map of a defeated country.
The army consumes every blade of grass in the valley,
every tree, every stream, every village,
every crossroad, every shack, every book, every graveyard.

His intact head
swivels around, to view the landscape of body
as if in dismay.

"For sixteen weeks I lived. For sixteen weeks
I took into myself nothing but the milk of my mother
who rolled on her side for me,
for my brothers and sisters. Only five hours roasting,
and this body so quickly dwindles away to nothing."

By itself, isolated on this plywood,
among this puzzle of foregone possibilities,
his intact head seems to want affection.
Without knowing that I will do it,
I reach out and scratch his jaw,
and I stroke him behind his ears,
as if he might suddenly purr from his cooked head.

"When I stroke your pig's ears,
and scratch the striped leather of your jowls,
the furrow between the sockets of your eyes,
I take into myself, and digest,
wheat that grew between
the Tigris and the Euphrates rivers.

"And I take into myself the flint carving tool,
and the savannah, and hairs in the tail
of Eohippus, and fingers of bamboo,
and Hannibal's elephant, and Hannibal,
and everything that lived before us, everything born,
exalted, and dead, and historians
who carved in the Old Kingdom
when the wall had not heard about China."

I speak these words
into the ear of the Stone Age pig, the Abraham
pig, the ocean pig, the Achilles pig,
and into the ears
of the fire pig that will eat our bodies up.

"Fire, brother and father,
twelve of us, in our different skins, older and younger,
opened your skin together
and tore your body apart, and took it
into our bodies."

The Blue Wing

She was all around me
like a rainy day,
and though I walked bareheaded
I was not wet. I walked
on a bare path
singing light songs
about women.

A blue wing tilts at the edge of the sea.

The wreck of the small
airplane sleeps
drifted to the high-tide line,
tangled in seaweed, green
glass from the sea.

The tiny skeleton inside
remembers the falter of engines, the cry
without answer,
the long dying
into and out of the sea.

Kicking the Leaves

1

Kicking the leaves, October, as we walk home together
from the game, in Ann Arbor,
on a day the color of soot, rain in the air;
I kick at the leaves of maples,
reds of seventy different shades, yellow
like old paper; and poplar leaves, fragile and pale;
and elm leaves, flags of a doomed race.
I kick at the leaves, making a sound I remember
as the leaves swirl upward from my boot
and flutter; and I remember
Octobers walking to school in Connecticut,
wearing corduroy knickers that swished
with a sound like leaves; and a Sunday buying
a cup of cider at a roadside stand
on a dirt road in New Hampshire; and kicking the leaves,
autumn 1955 in Massachusetts, knowing
my father would die when the leaves were gone.

2

Each fall in New Hampshire, on the farm
where my mother grew up, a girl in the country,
my grandfather and grandmother
finished the autumn work, taking the last vegetables in
from the cold fields, canning, storing roots and apples
in the cellar under the kitchen. Then my grandfather
raked leaves against the house

as the final chore of autumn.
One November I drove up from college to see them.
We pulled big rakes, as we did when we hayed in summer,
pulling the leaves against the granite foundations
around the house, on every side of the house,
and then, to keep them in place, we cut spruce boughs
and laid them across the leaves,
green on red, until the house
was tucked up, ready for snow
that would freeze the leaves in tight, like a stiff skirt.
Then we puffed through the shed door,
taking off boots and overcoats, slapping our hands,
and sat in the kitchen, rocking, and drank
black coffee my grandmother made,
three of us sitting together, silent, in gray November.

3

One Saturday when I was little, before the war,
my father came home at noon from his half day at the office
and wore his Bates sweater, black on red,
with the crossed hockey sticks on it, and raked beside me
in the backyard, and tumbled in the leaves
with me, and carried me laughing, my hair
full of leaves, to the kitchen window
where my mother could see us, and smile, and motion
to set me down, afraid I would fall and be hurt.

4

Kicking the leaves today, as we walk home together
from the game, among crowds of people
with their bright pennants, as many and bright as leaves,
my daughter's hair is the red-yellow color
of birch leaves, and she is tall like a birch,
growing up, fifteen, growing older; and my son
flamboyant as maple, twenty,
visits from college, and walks ahead of us, his step
springing, impatient to travel
the woods of the earth. Now I watch them
from a pile of leaves beside this clapboard house
in Ann Arbor, across from the school
where they learned to read,
as their shapes grow small with distance, waving,
and I know that I
diminish, not they, as I go first
into the leaves, taking
the way they will follow, Octobers and years from now.

5

This year the poems came back, when the leaves fell.
Kicking the leaves, I heard the leaves tell stories,
remembering, and therefore looking ahead, and building
the house of dying. I looked up into the maples
and found them, the vowels of bright desire.
I thought they had gone forever

while the bird sang *I love you, I love you*
and shook its black head
from side to side, and its red eye with no lid,
through years of winter, cold
as the taste of chickenwire, the music of cinderblock.

6

Kicking the leaves, I uncover the lids of graves.
My grandfather died at seventy-seven, in March
when the sap was running; and I remember my father
twenty years ago,
coughing himself to death at fifty-two in the house
in the suburbs. Oh, how we flung
leaves in the air! How they tumbled and fluttered around us
like slowly cascading water, when we walked together
in Hamden, before the war, when Johnson's Pond
had not surrendered to houses, the two of us
hand in hand, and in the wet air the smell of leaves
burning;
and in six years I will be fifty-two.

7

Now I fall, now I leap and fall
to feel the leaves crush under my body, to feel my body
buoyant in the ocean of leaves, the night of them,
night heaving with death and leaves, rocking like the ocean.
Oh, this delicious falling into the arms of leaves,
into the soft laps of leaves!
Face down, I swim into the leaves, feathery,
breathing the acrid odor of maple, swooping
in long glides to the bottom of October —
where the farm lies curled against winter, and soup steams
its breath of onion and carrot
onto damp curtains and windows; and past the windows
I see the tall bare maple trunks and branches, the oak
with its few brown weathery remnant leaves,
and the spruce trees, holding their green.
Now I leap and fall, exultant, recovering
from death — on account of death, in accord with the dead —
the smell and taste of leaves again,
and the pleasure, the only long pleasure, of taking a place
in the story of leaves.

The Table

Walking back to the farm from the depot,
Riley slapped flies with his tail.
Twilight. Crickets scraped
in the green standing hay by the road.
The voice of my grandfather
spoke through a motion of gnats.
I held his hand. I entered
the sway of a horse.
                              At the brown table
I propped books on each other.
All morning in the room my skin
took into itself small discs
of coolness.
Then I walked in the cut hayfield
by the barn, and lay alone
in the valley of noon heat,
in the village of little sounds.
Grasshoppers
tickled my neck and I let them.
I turned into the other world
that lives in the air. Clouds passed
like motes.
                       My grandfather
clanked up the road on his mowing machine,
behind Riley dark with sweat.
I ran to the barn
and carried a bucket of water

to the loose jaws working
in the dark stall. For lunch
I sliced an onion.
Then we raked hay into mounds
and my grandfather pitched it up
where I tucked it in place on the hayrack.
My skin dried in the sun. Wind
caught me in clover.
The slow ride
back to the barn, I dangled
legs over split-pole rails
while my grandfather talked forever
in a voice that wrapped me around
with love that asked for nothing.
In my room I drank well water
that whitened the sides of a tumbler
and coolness gathered like dark
inside my stomach.
                              This morning
I walk to the shaded bedroom and lean
on the drop-leaf table.
                          The table hums
a song to itself without sense
and I hear the voice of the heaving
ribs of Riley
and grasshoppers
haying the fields of the air.

Maple Syrup

August, goldenrod blowing. We walk
into the graveyard, to find
my grandfather's grave. Ten years ago
I came here last, bringing
marigolds from the round garden
outside the kitchen.
I didn't know you then.
                           We walk
among carved names that go with photographs
on top of the piano at the farm:
Keneston, Wells, Currier, Batchelder, Buck.
We pause at the new grave
of Grace Fenton, my grandfather's
sister. Last summer
we called on her at the nursing home,
eighty-seven, and nodding
in a blue housedress. We cannot find
my grandfather's grave.
                           Back at the house
where no one lives, we potter
and explore the back chamber
where everything comes to rest: spinning wheels,
pretty boxes, quilts,
bottles, books, albums of postcards.
Then with a flashlight we descend
frail steps to the root cellar — black,
cobwebby, huge,
with dirt floors and fieldstone walls,

and above the walls, holding the hewn
sills of the house, enormous
granite foundation stones.
Past the empty bins
for squash, apples, carrots, and potatoes,
we discover the shelves for canning, a few
pale pints
of tomato left, and — what
is this? — syrup, maple syrup
in a quart jar, syrup
my grandfather made twenty-five
years ago
for the last time.
                              I remember
coming to the farm in March
in sugaring time, as a small boy.
He carried the pails of sap, sixteen-quart
buckets, dangling from each end
of a wooden yoke
that lay across his shoulders, and emptied them
into a vat in the saphouse
where fire burned day and night
for a week.
                        Now the saphouse
tilts, nearly to the ground,
like someone exhausted
to the point of death, and next winter
when snow piles three feet thick

on the roofs of the cold farm,
the saphouse will shudder and slide
with the snow to the ground.
                              Today
we take my grandfather's last
quart of syrup
upstairs, holding it gingerly,
and we wash off twenty-five years
of dirt, and we pull
and pry the lid up, cutting the stiff,
dried rubber gasket, and dip our fingers
in, you and I both, and taste
the sweetness, you for the first time,
the sweetness preserved, of a dead man
in the kitchen he left
when his body slid
like anyone's into the ground.

Old Roses

White roses, tiny and old, flare among thorns
by the barn door.
                        For a hundred years
under the June elm, under the gaze
of seven generations,
                        they lived briefly
like this, in the month of roses,
                        by the fields
stout with corn, or with clover and timothy
making thick hay,
                        grown over, now,
with milkweed, sumac, paintbrush.
                        Old
roses survive
winter drifts, the melt in April, August
parch,
        and men and women
who sniffed roses in spring and called them pretty
as we call them now,
                        walking beside the barn
on a day that perishes.

Names of Horses

All winter your brute shoulders strained against collars, padding
and steerhide over the ash hames, to haul
sledges of cordwood for drying through spring and summer,
for the Glenwood stove next winter, and for the simmering range.

In April you pulled cartloads of manure to spread on the fields,
dark manure of Holsteins, and knobs of your own clustered with
      oats.
All summer you mowed the grass in meadow and hayfield, the
      mowing machine
clacketing behind you, while the sun walked high in the morning;

and after noon's heat, you pulled a clawed rake through the same
      acres,
gathering stacks, and dragged the wagon from stack to stack,
and the built hayrack back, up hill to the chaffy barn,
three loads of hay a day from standing grass in the morning.

Sundays you trotted the two miles to church with the light load
of a leather quartertop buggy, and grazed in the sound of hymns.
Generation on generation, your neck rubbed the window sill
of the stall, smoothing the wood as the sea smooths glass.

When you were old and lame, when your shoulders hurt
      bending to graze,
one October the man who fed you and kept you, and harnessed
      you every morning,
led you through corn stubble to sandy ground above Eagle Pond,
and dug a hole beside you where you stood shuddering in your
      skin,

and laid the shotgun's muzzle in the boneless hollow behind your
      ear,
and fired the slug into your brain, and felled you into your grave,
shoveling sand to cover you, setting goldenrod upright above you,
where by next summer a dent in the ground made your
      monument.

For a hundred and fifty years, in the pasture of dead horses,
roots of pine trees pushed through the pale curves of your ribs,
yellow blossoms flourished above you in autumn, and in winter
frost heaved your bones in the ground — old toilers, soil makers:

O Roger, Mackerel, Riley, Ned, Nellie, Chester, Lady Ghost.

Ox-Cart Man

In October of the year,
he counts potatoes dug from the brown field,
counting the seed, counting
the cellar's portion out,
and bags the rest on the cart's floor.

He packs wool sheared in April, honey
in combs, linen, leather
tanned from deerhide,
and vinegar in a barrel
hooped by hand at the forge's fire.

He walks by his ox's head, ten days
to Portsmouth Market, and sells potatoes,
and the bag that carried potatoes,
flaxseed, birch brooms, maple sugar, goose
feathers, yarn.

When the cart is empty he sells the cart.
When the cart is sold he sells the ox,
harness and yoke, and walks
home, his pockets heavy
with the year's coin for salt and taxes,

and at home by fire's light in November cold
stitches new harness
for next year's ox in the barn,
and carves the yoke, and saws planks
building the cart again.

Flies

A fly slept on the field of a green curtain.
I sat by my grandmother's side, and rubbed her head
as if I could comfort her. Ninety-seven years.
Kate's eyes stayed closed, her mouth open,
and she gasped in her blue nightgown — pale blue,
washed a thousand times. Now her face went white,
and her breath slowed until it seemed to stop.
Then she gasped again, and pink returned to her face.
Between the roof of her mouth and her tongue,
strands of spittle wavered as she breathed. A nurse
shook her head over my grandmother's sore mouth
and fetched a glass of water, a spoon, and a flyswatter.
My grandmother choked on a spoonful of water
and the nurse swatted the fly.

                              In Connecticut suburbs
where I grew up, and in Ann Arbor, there were houses
with small leaded panes, where Formica shone
in the kitchens, and hardwood in closets under paired
leather boots. Carpets lay thick underfoot in bedrooms,
bright, clean, with no dust or hair in them.
Florist's flowers leaned from Waterford vases
for the Saturday dinner party. Even in houses like these,
the housefly wandered and paused — and I listened
for the buzz of its wings and its tiny feet, as it struggled
among cut flowers and bumped into leaded panes.

In the afternoon my mother took over
at my grandmother's side in the Peabody Home,
while I went back to the farm. I napped in the room
my mother and grandmother were born in.
At night we assembled beside her. Her shallow, rapid
breath rasped, and her eyes jerked, and the nurse
found no pulse, as her strength concentrated wholly
on half an inch of lung space, and she coughed faintly,
quick coughs, like fingertips on a ledge. Her daughters
stood by the bed — solemn in the slow evening,
in the shallows of after-supper — Caroline, Nan, and Lucy,
her eldest daughter, seventy-two, who held
her hand to help her die, as twenty years ago
she did the same for my father. Then Kate's breath slowed
again, as it did all day. Pink vanished from cheeks
we had kissed so often, nostrils quivered,
and she breathed one more quick breath.
Her mouth twisted sharply, as if she spoke
a word we couldn't hear.

                        She lay in a casket of gray linen
at Chadwick's Funeral Parlor in New London,
on the second floor over the I.O.O.F. Her fine hair
lay combed on the pillow. Her teeth in, her mouth
closed, she looked the way she used to look,
except that her face was tinted, tanned
as if she worked in the fields. The air was so still
it had bars. I imagined a fly wandering in,

through these dark-curtained windows, to land
on my grandmother's nose.

                        At the Andover graveyard,
Astroturf covered the dirt next to the dug shaft.
By the hole, Mr. Jones said a prayer,
who preached at the South Danbury Church
when my grandmother still played the organ.
He raised his narrow voice, which gave itself over
to August and blue air, and told us that Kate
in heaven "will keep on growing . . . and growing . . .
and growing . . ." and he stopped abruptly
as if the sky abandoned him.

                        I walked by myself
in the barn where I spent summers
next to my grandfather Wesley. In the tie-up a chaff
of flies roiled in the leather air, as he milked
his Holsteins morning and night, his bald head
pressed sweating into their sides, fat female
Harlequins. Their black-and-white tails
swept back and forth, stirring the flies up. His voice
spoke pieces he learned for the Lyceum,
and I listened crouched on a three-legged stool
as his hands kept time *strp strp* with alternate streams
of hot milk, the sound softer as milk foamed
to the pail's top. In the tie-up the spiders
feasted like Nero. Each April he broomed the webs out

and whitewashed the wood, but spiders and flies
came back, generation on generation — like the cattle,
mothers and daughters, for a hundred and fifty years,
until my grandfather Wesley's heart flapped in his chest.
One by one the slow Holsteins climbed the ramp
into a cattle truck.

                              In the kitchen with its bare
hardwood floor, my grandmother stood
by the clock's mirror to braid her hair every morning.
She looked out the window toward Kearsarge,
and said, "Mountain's real pretty today,"
or, "Can't see the mountain too good today."
She fought the flies all summer. She shut
the screen door quickly, but flies gathered
on canisters, on the clockface, on the range
when the fire was out, on set-tubs, tables, chairs.
Flies buzzed on cooling lard, when my grandmother
made doughnuts. Flies lit on a drip of jam
before she could wipe it up. Flies whirled
over simmering beans, in the steam
of maple syrup. My grandmother fretted,
and took good aim with a flyswatter,
and hung strips of sticky paper behind the range,
where nobody would tangle her hair.
She gave me a penny for every ten I killed.
All day with my mesh flyswatter I patrolled
kitchen and dining room, living room,

even the dead air of the parlor. Though I killed
every fly in the house by bedtime,
when Kate washed the hardwood floor,
by morning their sons and cousins
assembled in the kitchen, like the woodchucks
my grandfather shot in the vegetable garden,
that doubled and returned; like the deer
that watched for a hundred and fifty years
from the brush on Ragged Mountain,
and when my grandfather died,
stalked down the mountainside to graze
among peas and beans.

                              We live in their house
with our books and pictures, gazing each morning
at blue Kearsarge. We live in the house left behind.
We sleep in the bed where they whispered together
at night. One morning I woke hearing a voice from sleep:
"The blow of the axe resides in the acorn."
I got out of bed and drank cold water in the dark
morning from the sink's dipper
at the window under the leaning maple,
and a fly woke buzzing beside me,
and swept over set-tubs and range,
one of the hundred-thousandth generation.
I planned long ago I would live here.

The Town of Hill

Back of the dam, under
a flat pad

of water, church
bells ring

in the ears of lilies,
a child's swing

curls in the current
of a yard, horned

pout sleep
in a green

mailbox, and
a boy walks

from a screened
porch beneath

the man-shaped
leaves of an oak

down the street looking
at the town

of Hill that water
covered forty

years ago,
and the screen

door shuts
under dream water.

Great Day in the Cows' House

In the dark tie-up seven huge Holsteins
lower their heads to feed, chained loosely to old saplings
with whitewashed bark still on them.
They are long dead; they survive, in the great day
that cancels the successiveness of creatures.
Now she stretches her wrinkly neck, her turnip eye
rolls in her skull, she sucks up breath,
and stretching her long mouth mid-chew she expels:
mm-mmm-mmmmm-mmmmmmmm-ugghwanchhh.
— Sweet bellowers enormous and interchangeable,
your dolorous ululations
swell out barnsides, fill spaces inside haymows,
resound down valleys. Moos of revenant cattle
shake ancient timbers and timbers still damp with sap.

Now it is warm, late June. The old man strokes
white braids of milk, *strp strp,* from ruminant beasts
with hipbones like tentpoles, the rough
black-and-white hanging crudely upon them.
Now he tilts back his head to recite a poem
about an old bachelor who loves a chicken named Susan.
His voice grows loud with laughter and emphasis
in the silent tie-up where old noises gather.

Now a tail lifts to waterfall huge and yellow
or an enormous flop presses out. Done milking, he lifts

with his hoe a leather-hinged board
to scrape manure onto the pile underneath, in April
carted for garden and fieldcorn.
                                        The cows in their house
decree the seasons; spring seeds corn,
summer hays, autumn fences, and winter saws ice
from Eagle Pond, sledging it up hill to pack it away
in sawdust; through August's parch and Indian summer
great chunks of the pond float in the milkshed tank.

❧

Pull down the spiderwebs! Whitewash the tie-up!
In the great day there is also the odor of poverty
and anxiety over the Agricultural Inspector's visit.

❧

They are long dead; they survive, in the great day
of August, to convene afternoon and morning
for milking. Now they graze Ragged Mountain: —
steep sugarbush, little mountain valleys and brooks,
high clovery meadows, slate-colored lowbush blueberries.
When grass is sweetest they are slow to leave it;
late afternoons he spends hours searching.
He knows their secret places; he listens for one peal
of a cowbell carried on a breeze; he calls:
"Ke-bosh, ke-bo-o-sh, ke-bosh, ke-bosh . . ."
He climbs dry creekbeds and old logging roads
or struggles up needle-banks pulling on fir branches.

He hacks with his jackknife a chunk of sprucegum
oozing from bark and softens it in his cheek-pouch
for chewing.
                    Then he pushes through hemlock's gate
to join the society of Holsteins; they look up from grass
as if mildly surprised, and file immediately downwards.

☙

Late in October after the grass freezes
the cattle remain in their stalls, twice a day loosed
to walk stiff-legged to the watering trough
from which the old man lifts a white lid of ice.
Twice a day he shovels ensilage into their stalls
and shakes hay down from the loft, stuffing a forkful
under each steaming nose.
                              In late winter,
one after one, the pink-white udders
dry out as new calves swell their mothers' bellies.
Now these vessels of hugeness bear, one after one,
skinny-limbed small Holsteins eager to suck
the bounty of freshening. Now he climbs to the barn
in boots and overalls, two sweaters,
a cloth cap, and somebody's old woolen coat;
now he parts the calf from its mother after feeding,
and strips the udder clean,
to rejoice in the sweet frothing tonnage of milk.

☙

Now in April, when snow remains on the north side
of boulders and sugarmaples, and green
starts from wet earth in open places the sun touches,
he unchains the cows one morning after milking
and lopes past them to open the pasture gate.
Now he returns whooping and slapping their buttocks
to set them to pasture again, and they are free
to wander eating all day long. Now these wallowing
big-eyed calf-makers, bone-rafters for leather,
awkward arks, cud-chewing lethargic mooers,
roll their enormous heads, trot, gallop, bounce,
cavort, stretch, leap, and bellow —
as if everything heavy and cold vanished at once
and cow spirits floated
weightless as clouds in the great day's windy April.

When his neighbor discovers him at eighty-seven, his head
leans into the side of his last Holstein;
she has kicked the milkpail over, and blue milk drains
through floorboards onto the manure pile in the great day.

Old Timers' Day

When the tall puffy
figure wearing number
nine starts
late for the fly ball,
laboring forward
like a lame truckhorse
startled by a gartersnake,
— this old fellow
whose body we remember
as sleek and nervous
as a filly's —

and barely catches it
in his glove's
tip, we rise
and applaud weeping:
On a green field
we observe the ruin
of even the bravest
body, as Odysseus
wept to glimpse
among shades the shadow
of Achilles.

Mr. Wakeville on Interstate 90

"Now I will abandon the route of my life
as my shadowy wives abandon me, taking my children.
I will stop somewhere. I will park in a summer street
where the days tick like metal in the stillness.
I will rent the room over Bert's Modern Barbershop
where the TO LET sign leans in the plateglass window;
or I will buy the brown BUNGALOW FOR SALE.

"I will work forty hours a week clerking at the paintstore.
On Fridays I will cash my paycheck at Six Rivers Bank
and stop at Harvey's Market and talk with Harvey.
Walking on Maple Street I will speak to everyone.
At basketball games I will cheer for my neighbors' sons.
I will watch my neighbors' daughters grow up, marry,
raise children. The joints of my fingers will stiffen.

"There will be no room inside me for other places.
I will attend funerals regularly and weddings.
I will chat with the mailman when he comes on Saturdays.
I will shake my head when I hear of the florist
who drops dead in the greenhouse over a flat of pansies;
I spoke with her only yesterday.
When lawyer elopes with babysitter I will shake my head.

"When Harvey's boy enlists in the Navy
I will wave goodbye at the Trailways depot with the others.

I will vote Democratic; I will vote Republican.
I will applaud the valedictorian at graduation
and wish her well as she goes away to the university
and weep as she goes away. I will live in a steady joy;
I will exult in the ecstasy of my concealment."

Moon Clock

Like an oarless boat through midnight's watery
ghosthouse, through lumens and shallows
of shadow, under smoky light that the full moon
reflects from snowfields to ceilings, I drift
on January's tide from room to room, pausing
by the wooden clock with its pendulum that keeps
the beat like a heart certainly beating, to wait
for the pause allowing passage
to repose's shore — where all waves halt
upreared and stony as the moon's Mycenaean lions.

The Impossible Marriage

The bride disappears. After twenty minutes of searching
we discover her in the cellar, vanishing against a pillar
in her white gown and her skin's original pallor.
When we guide her back to the altar, we find the groom
in his slouch hat, open shirt, and untended beard
withdrawn to the belltower with the healthy young sexton
from whose comradeship we detach him with difficulty.
O never in all the meetinghouses and academies
of compulsory Democracy and free-thinking Calvinism
will these poets marry! — O pale, passionate
anchoret of Amherst! O reticent kosmos of Brooklyn!

Edward's Anecdote

"Late one night she told me.
    We'd come home from a party
where she drank more wine
    than usual, from nervousness

"I suppose. I was astonished,
    which is typical,
and her lover of course
    was my friend. My naïveté

"served their purposes: What
    you don't know beats your head in.
After weeping for an hour or so
    I tried screaming.

"Then I quieted down;
    then I broke her grandmother's
teapot against the pantry brickwork,
    which helped a bit.

"She kept apologizing
    as she walked back and forth,
chainsmoking. I hated her,
    and thought how beautiful

"she looked as she paced,
    which started me weeping again.
Old puzzlements began to solve
      themselves: the errand

"that took all afternoon;
    the much-explained excursion
to stay with a college roommate
    at a hunting lodge

"without a telephone;
    and of course the wrong numbers.
Then my masochistic mind
    printed Kodacolors

"of my friend and my wife
    arranged in bed together.
When I looked out the window,
    I saw the sky going

"pale with dawn; soon the children
    would wake: Thinking of them
started me weeping again.
    I felt exhausted, and

"I wanted to sleep neither
     with her nor without her,
which made me remember:
     When I was a child we knew

"a neighbor named Mr. Jaspers —
     an ordinary
gray and agreeable
     middle-aged businessman who

"joked with the neighborhood
     children when he met us on
the street, giving us pennies,
     except for once a year

"when he got insanely drunk
     and the police took him.
One time he beat his year-old
     daughter with a broomstick,

"breaking a rib bone, and as
     she screamed she kept crawling
back to her father: Where else
     should she look for comfort?"

Fête

Festival lights go on
in villages throughout
   the province, from Toe
Harbor, past the
   Elbow Lakes, to Eyelid Hill
when you touch me, there.

The Day I Was Older

The Clock
The clock on the parlor wall, stout as a mariner's clock,
disperses the day. All night it tolls the half-hour
and the hour's number with resolute measure,
approaching the poles and crossing the equator
over fathoms of sleep. Warm
in the dark next to your breathing,
below the thousand favored stars, I feel
horns of gray water heave
underneath us, and the ship's pistons
pound as the voyage continues over the limited sea.

The News
After tending the fire, making coffee, and pouring milk
for cats, I sit in a blue chair each morning,
reading obituaries in the *Boston Globe*
for the mean age; today there is MANUFACTURER CONCORD 53,
EX-CONGRESSMAN SAUGUS 80 — and I read
that Emily Farr is dead, after a long illness in Oregon.
Once in an old house we talked for an hour, while a coal fire
brightened in November twilight and wavered
our shadows high on the wall
until our eyes fixed on each other. Thirty years ago.

The Pond
We lie by the pond on a late August afternoon
as a breeze from low hills in the west stiffens water
and agitates birch leaves yellowing above us.
You set down your book
and lift your eyes to white trunks tilting from shore.
A mink scuds through ferns; an acorn tumbles.
Soon we will turn to our daily business.
You do not know that I am watching, taking pleasure
in your breasts that rise and fall as you breathe.
Then I see mourners gathered by an open grave.

The Day
Last night at suppertime I outlived my father, enduring
the year, month, day, hour, and moment
when he lay back on a hospital bed in the guest room
among cylinders of oxygen — mouth open, nostrils and pale
blue lips fixed unquivering. Father of my name,
father of long fingers, I remember your dark hair
and your face almost unwrinkled. Now I have waked
more mornings to frost whitening the grass,
read the newspaper more times, and stood more times,
my hand on a doorknob without opening the door.

The Cup

From the Studebaker's back seat, on our Sunday drives,
I watched her earrings sway. Then I walked up hill
beside an old man carrying buckets
under birches on an August day. Striding at noontime,
I looked at wheat and at river cities. In the crib
my daughter sighed opening her eyes. I kissed the cheek
of my father dying. By the pond an acorn fell.
You listening here, you reading these words as I write them,
I offer this cup to you: Though we drink
from this cup every day, we will never drink it dry.

The Baseball Players

Against the bright
grass the white-knickered
players tense, seize,
and attend. A moment
ago, outfielders
and infielders adjusted
their clothing, glanced
at the sun and settled
forward, hands on knees;
the pitcher walked back
of the hill, established
his cap and returned;
the catcher twitched
a forefinger; the batter
rotated his bat
in a slow circle. But now
they pause: wary,
exact, suspended —

                while
abiding moonrise
lightens the angel
of the overgrown
garden, and Walter Blake
Adams, who died
at fourteen, waits
under the footbridge.

When the Young Husband

When the young husband picked up his friend's pretty wife
in the taxi one block from her townhouse for their
first lunch together, in a hotel dining room
                with a room key in his pocket,

midtown traffic gridlocked and was abruptly still.
For one moment before klaxons started honking,
a prophetic voice spoke in his mind's ear despite
                his pulse's erotic thudding.

"The misery you undertake this afternoon
will accompany you to the ends of your lives.
She knew what she did when she agreed to this lunch,
                although she will not admit it;

"and you've constructed your playlet a thousand times:
cocktails, an omelet, wine; the revelation
of a room key; the elevator rising as
                the penis elevates; the skin

"flushed, the door fumbled at, the handbag dropped; the first
kiss with open mouths, nakedness, swoon, thrust-and-catch;
endorphins followed by endearments; a brief nap;
                another fit; restoration

"of clothes, arrangements for another encounter,
the taxi back, and the furtive kiss of goodbye.
Then, by turn: tears, treachery, anger, betrayal;
                marriages and houses destroyed;

"small children abandoned and inconsolable,
their foursquare estates disestablished forever;
the unreadable advocates; the wretchedness
                    of passion outworn; anguished nights

"sleepless in a bare room; whiskey, meth, cocaine; new
love, essayed in loneliness with miserable
strangers, that comforts nothing but skin; hours with sons
                    and daughters studious always

"to maintain distrust; the daily desire to die
and the daily agony of the requirement
to survive, until only the quarrel endures."
                    Prophecy stopped; traffic started.

Prophecy

from *The One Day*

I will strike down wooden houses; I will burn aluminum
clapboard skin; I will strike down garages
where crimson Toyotas sleep side by side; I will explode
palaces of gold, silver, and alabaster: — the summer
great house and its folly together. Where shopping malls
spread plywood and plaster out, and roadhouses
serve steak and potatoskins beside Alaska king crab;
where triangular flags proclaim tribes of identical campers;
where airplanes nose to tail exhale kerosene,
weeds and ashes will drowse in continual twilight.

I reject the old house and the new car; I reject
Tory and Whig together; I reject the argument
that modesty of ambition is sensible because the bigger
they are the harder they fall; I reject Waterford;
I reject the five-and-dime; I reject Romulus and Remus;
I reject Martha's Vineyard and the slamdunk contest;
I reject leaded panes; I reject the appointment made
at the tennis net or on the seventh green; I reject
the Professional Bowlers Tour; I reject matchboxes;
I reject purple bathrooms with purple soap in them.

Men who lie awake worrying about taxes, vomiting
at dawn, whose hands shake as they administer Valium, —
skin will peel from the meat of their thighs.
Armies that march all day with elephants past pyramids
and roll pulling missiles past generals weary of saluting

and past president-emperors splendid in cloth-of-gold, —
soft rumps of armies will dissipate in rain. Where square
miles of corn waver in Minnesota, where tobacco ripens
in Carolina and apples in New Hampshire, where wheat
turns Kansas green, where pulpmills stink in Oregon, —

dust will blow in the darkness and cactus die
before it flowers. Where skiers wait for chairlifts,
wearing money, low raspberries will part rib bones.
Where the drive-in church raises a chromium cross,
dandelions and milkweed will straggle through blacktop.
I will strike from the ocean with waves afire;
I will strike from the hill with rainclouds of lava;
I will strike from darkened air
with melanoma in the shape of decorative hexagonals.
I will strike down embezzlers and eaters of snails.

I reject Japanese smoked oysters, potted chrysanthemums
allowed to die, Tupperware parties, Ronald McDonald,
Kaposi's sarcoma, the Taj Mahal, Holsteins wearing
electronic necklaces, the Algonquin, Tunisian aqueducts,
Phi Beta Kappa keys, the Hyatt Embarcadero, carpenters
jogging on the median, and betrayal that engorges
the corrupt heart longing for criminal surrender.
I reject shadows in the corner of the atrium
where Phyllis or Phoebe speaks with Billy or Marc
who says that afternoons are best although not reliable.

Your children will wander looting the shopping malls
for forty years, suffering for your idleness,
until the last dwarf body rots in a parking lot.
I will strike down lobbies and restaurants in motels
carpeted with shaggy petrochemicals
from Maine to Hilton Head, from the Skagit to Tucson.
I will strike down hang gliders, wiry adventurous boys;
their thigh bones will snap, their brains
slide from their skulls. I will strike down
families cooking wildboar in New Mexico backyards.

Then landscape will clutter with incapable machinery,
acres of vacant airplanes and schoolbuses, ploughs
with seedlings sprouting and turning brown through colters.
Unlettered dwarves will burrow for warmth and shelter
in the caves of dynamos and Plymouths, dying
of old age at seventeen. Tribes wandering
in the wilderness of their ignorant desolation,
who suffer from your idleness, will burn your illuminated
missals to warm their rickety bodies.
Terrorists assemble plutonium because you are idle

and industrious. The whippoorwill shrivels
and the pickerel chokes under the government of self-love.
Vacancy burns air so that you strangle without oxygen
like rats in a biologist's bell jar. The living god sharpens
the scythe of my prophecy to strike down red poppies

and blue cornflowers. When priests and policemen
strike my body's match, Jehovah will flame out;
Jehovah will suck air from the vents of bombshelters.
Therefore let the Buick swell until it explodes;
therefore let anorexia starve and bulimia engorge.

When Elzira leaves the house wearing her tennis dress
and drives her black Porsche to meet Abraham,
quarrels, returns to husband and children, and sobs
asleep, drunk, unable to choose among them, —
lawns and carpets will turn into tar together
with lovers, husbands, and children.
Fat will boil in the sacs of children's clear skin.
I will strike down the nations, astronauts and judges;
I will strike down Babylon, I will strike acrobats,
I will strike algae and the white birches.

Because professors of law teach ethics in dumbshow,
let the colonel become president; because chief executive
officers and commissars collect down for pillows,
let the injustice of cities burn city and suburb;
let the countryside burn; let the pineforests of Maine
explode like a kitchenmatch and the Book of Kells turn
ash in a microsecond; let oxen and athletes
flash into grease: — I return to Appalachian rocks;
I shall eat bread; I shall prophesy through millennia
of Jehovah's day until the sky reddens over cities:

Then houses will burn, even houses of alabaster;
the sky will disappear like a scroll rolled up
and hidden in a cave from the industries of idleness.
Mountains will erupt and vanish, becoming deserts,
and the sea wash over the sea's lost islands
and the earth split open like a corpse's gassy
stomach and the sun turn as black as a widow's skirt
and the full moon grow red with blood swollen inside it
and stars fall from the sky like wind-blown apples, —
while Babylon's managers burn in the rage of the Lamb.

Tubes

"Up, down, good, bad," said
the man with the tubes
up his nose, "there is lots
of variety . . .
However, notions
of balance between
extremes of fortune
are stupid! — or at
best unobservant."
He watched as the nurse
fed pellets into
the green nozzle that
stuck from his side. "Mm,"
said the man. "Good. Yum.
Next time more basil . . .
When a long-desired
baby is born, what
joy! More happiness
than we find in sex,
more than we take in
success, revenge, or
money. Should the same
infant die, would you
measure the horror
on the same rule? Grief
weighs down the seesaw;
joy cannot budge it."

The Peepers, the Woodshed

Mount Kearsarge shines with ice; from hemlock branches
snow slides onto snow; no stream, creek, or river
                budges but remains still. Tonight
                        we carry armloads of logs

from woodshed to Glenwood and build up the fire
that keeps the coldest night outside our windows.
                Sit by the woodstove, Jane Kenyon,
                        while I bring glasses of white,

and we'll talk, passing the time, about weather
without pretending that we can alter it.
                Storms stop when they stop, no sooner,
                        leaving the birches glossy

with ice and bent glittering to rimy ground.
We'll avoid the programmed weatherman grinning
                from the box, cheerful with tempest,
                        and take the day as it comes,

one day at a time, the way everyone says.
These hours are the best because we hold them close
                in our uxorious nation.
                        Soon we'll walk — when days turn fair

and frost stays off — over old roads, listening
for peepers as spring comes on, never to miss
                the day's offering of pleasure
                        for the government of two.

T.R.

Granted that what we summon is absurd:
Mustaches and the stick, the New York fake
In cowboy costume grinning for the sake
Of cameras that always just occurred;
Granted that his Rough Riders fought a third-
Rate army badly run, to make
Headlines to fatten Hearst: that one can take
Trust-busting not exactly at its word;

Robinson, who was drunken and unread,
Received a letter with a White House frank.
To court the Muse, T.R. might well have killed her
And had her stuffed, yet here this mountebank
Chose to belaurel Robinson instead
Of famous men like Richard Watson Gilder.

Six Naps in One Day

1

In the nap there are numerous doors, boudoirs, a talking hall
of sisters who gesture underwater, and bricked-up memoirs
with closets inside. There are bikes and desks in the nap,

2

corridors of glory, water, and pots of ivy hooked to ceiling
or ocean floor. Apes play with papers on the busy desk
I swim up to, through laborious sleep water. Rex the butcher

3

wears a straw hat sleeping on sawdust. When the extinguished
U-boat, flapping bat wings, settles under millennial silt,
whose eyes gleam through the periscope? They are Regina's.

4

Two squadrons of black biplanes dogfight over the trenches
of nineteen seventeen, death's-heads graven on engine cowlings,
helmeted pilots' faces turned into skulls, and their bones

5

as shadowy blue as underwater feet in the shoestore x-ray.
The gibbon's cry hobbles on the wooded shore, like the cry
of this bed. He walks by the ocean's tide a thousand years

6

in his gown of claws and hair, a deposed king searching
for sleep's bosom and the tall queen of dunes: Regina
skulks hiding in salt grass — while the halt gibbon howls.

Nose

it is a snail
that hesitates on a hedge
under eucalyptus

it is a fist
it is a wooden propeller

it is an accurate nose
like an adding machine
powered by perfect electricity
yet it has no cord
it does not run on batteries

it is an observatory
for observing moons and planets
I watch it
revolve

it is a birchbark canoe
Abenakis paddle

it is the egg
of a demonstrable bird
do not sit on this nose
it might hatch

Scenic View

Every year the mountains
get paler and more distant —
trees less green, rock piles
disappearing — as emulsion
from a billion Kodaks
sucks color out.
In fifteen years
Monadnock and Kearsarge,
the Green Mountains
and the White, will turn
invisible, all
tint removed
atom by atom to albums
in Medford and Greenwich,
while over the valleys
the still intractable granite
rears with unseeable peaks
fatal to airplanes.

The Painted Bed

"Even when I danced erect
by the Nile's garden
I constructed Necropolis.

"Ten million fellaheen cells
of my body floated stones
to establish a white museum."

Grisly, foul, and terrific
is the speech of bones,
thighs and arms slackened

into desiccated sacs of flesh
hanging from an armature
where muscle was, and fat.

"I lie on the painted bed
diminishing, concentrated
on the journey I undertake

"to repose without pain
in the palace of darkness,
my body beside your body."

The Porcelain Couple

When Jane felt well enough for me to leave her
a whole day, I drove south by the river
to empty my mother's house in Connecticut.
I hurried from room to room, cellar to attic,
looking into a crammed storeroom, then turning
to discover a chest with five full drawers.
I labeled for shipping sofas and chairs,
bedroom sets, and tables; I wrapped figurines
and fancy teacups in paper, preserving
things she had cherished — and in late years dreaded
might go for a nickel at a sale on the lawn.
Everywhere I saw shelves and tabletops
covered with glass animals and music boxes.
In closets, decades of finery hung in dead air.
I swept ashtrays and blouses into plastic sacks,
and the green-gold dress she wore to Bermuda.
At the last moment I discovered and saved
a cut-glass tumbler, stained red at the top,
Lucy 1905 scripted on the stain. In the garage
I piled bags for the dump, then drove four hours
north with my hands tight on the steering wheel,
drank a beer looking through the day's mail,
and pitched into bed with Jane who slept fitfully.
When I woke, I rose as if from a drunken sleep
after looting a city and burning its temples.
All day, while I ate lunch or counted out pills,
I noticed the objects of our twenty years:

a blue vase, a candelabrum Jane carried on her lap
from the Baja, and the small porcelain box
from France I found under the tree one Christmas
where a couple in relief stretch out asleep,
like a catafalque, on the pastel double bed
of the box's top, both wearing pretty nightcaps.

The Ship Pounding

Each morning I made my way
among gangways, elevators,
and nurses' pods to Jane's room
to interrogate the grave helpers
who tended her through the night
while the ship's massive engines
kept its propellers turning.
Week after week, I sat by her bed
with black coffee and the *Globe*.
The passengers on this voyage
wore masks or cannulae
or dangled devices that dripped
chemicals into their wrists.
I believed that the ship
traveled to a harbor
of breakfast, work, and love.
I wrote: "When the infusions
are infused entirely, bone
marrow restored and lymphoblasts
remitted, I will take my wife,
bald as Michael Jordan,
back to our dog and day." Today,
months later at home, these
words turned up on my desk
as I listened in case Jane called
for help, or spoke in delirium,
ready to make the agitated
drive to Emergency again

for readmission to the huge
vessel that heaves water month
after month, without leaving
port, without moving a knot,
without arrival or destination,
its great engines pounding.

Without

we lived in a small island stone nation
without color under gray clouds and wind
distant the unlimited ocean acute
lymphoblastic leukemia without seagulls
or palm trees without vegetation
or animal life only barnacles and lead
colored moss that darkened when months did

hours days weeks months weeks days hours
the year endured without punctuation
february without ice winter sleet
snow melted recovered but nothing
without thaw although cold streams hurtled
no snowdrop or crocus rose no yellow
no red leaves of maple without october

no spring no summer no autumn no winter
no rain no peony thunder no woodthrush
the book was a thousand pages without commas
without mice oak leaves windstorms
no castles no plazas no flags no parrots
without carnival or the procession of relics
intolerable without brackets or colons

silence without color sound without smell
without apples without pork to rupture gnash
unpunctuated without churches uninterrupted
no orioles ginger noses no opera no

without fingers daffodils cheekbones
the body was a nation a tribe dug into stone
assaulted white blood broken to shards

provinces invaded bombed shot shelled
artillery sniper fire helicopter gunship
grenade burning murder landmine starvation
the ceasefire lasted forty-eight hours
then a shell exploded in a market
pain vomit neuropathy morphine nightmare
confusion the rack terror the vise

vincristine ara-c cytoxan vp-16
loss of memory loss of language losses
pneumocystis carinii pneumonia bactrim
foamless unmitigated sea without sea
delirium whipmarks of petechiae
multiple blisters of herpes zoster
and how are you doing today I am doing

one afternoon say the sun came out
moss took on greenishness leaves fell
the market opened a loaf of bread a sparrow
a bony dog wandered back sniffing a lath
it might be possible to take up a pencil
unwritten stanzas taken up and touched
beautiful terrible sentences unuttered

the sea unrelenting wave gray the sea
flotsam without islands broken crates
block after block the same house the mall
no cathedral no hobo jungle the same women
and men they longed to drink hayfields no
without dog or semicolon or village square
without monkey or lily without garlic

Letter with No Address

Your daffodils rose up
and collapsed in their yellow
bodies on the hillside
garden above the bricks
you laid out in sand, squatting
with pants pegged and face
masked like a beekeeper's
against the black flies.
Buttercups circle the planks
of the old wellhead
this May while your silken
gardener's body withers or moulds
in the Proctor graveyard.
I drive and talk to you crying
and come back to this house
to talk to your photographs.

There's news to tell you:
Maggie Fisher's pregnant.
I carried myself like an egg
at Abigail's birthday party
a week after you died,
as three-year-olds bounced
uproarious on a mattress.
Joyce and I met for lunch
at the mall and strolled weepily
through Sears and B. Dalton.

Today it's four weeks
since you lay on our painted bed
and I closed your eyes.
Yesterday I cut irises to set
in a pitcher on your grave;
today I brought a carafe
to fill it with fresh water.
I remember bone pain,
vomiting, delirium. I remember
pond afternoons.
                        My routine
is established: coffee;
the *Globe*; breakfast;
writing you this letter
at my desk. When I go to bed
to sleep after baseball,
Gus follows me into the bedroom
as he used to follow us.
Most of the time he flops
down in the parlor
with his head on his paws.

Once a week I drive to Tilton
to see Dick and Nan.
Nan doesn't understand much
but she knows you're dead;
I feel her fretting. The tune

of Dick and me talking
seems to console her.
                                  You know now
whether the soul survives death.
Or you don't. When you were dying
you said you didn't fear
punishment. We never dared
to speak of Paradise.
At five A.M., when I walk outside,
mist lies thick on hayfields.
By eight the air is clear,
cool, sunny with the pale yellow
light of mid-May. Kearsarge
rises huge and distinct,
each birch and balsam visible.
To the west the waters
of Eagle Pond waver
and flash through popples just
leafing out.
                    Always the weather,
writing its book of the world,
returns you to me.
Ordinary days were best,
when we worked over poems
in our separate rooms.
I remember watching you gaze
out the January window

into the garden of snow
and ice, your face rapt
as you imagined burgundy lilies.

Your presence in this house
is almost as enormous
and painful as your absence.
Driving home from Tilton,
I remember how you cherished
that vista with its center
the red door of a farmhouse
against green fields.

Are you past pity?
If you have consciousness now,
if something I can call
"you" has something
like "consciousness," I doubt
you remember the last days.
I play them over and over:
I lift your wasted body
onto the commode, your arms
looped around my neck, aiming
your bony bottom so that
it will not bruise on a rail.
Faintly you repeat,
"Momma, Momma."

                    Three times
today I drove to your grave.
Sometimes, coming back home
to our circular driveway,
I imagine you've returned
before me, bags of groceries upright
in the back of the Saab,
its trunk lid delicately raised
as if proposing an encounter,
dog-fashion, with the Honda.

Weeds and Peonies

Your peonies burst out, white as snow squalls,
with red flecks at their shaggy centers
in your border of prodigies by the porch.
I carry one magnanimous blossom indoors
and float it in a glass bowl, as you used to do.

Ordinary pleasures, contentment recollected,
blow like snow into the abandoned garden,
overcoming the daisies. Your blue coat
vanishes down Pond Road into imagined snowflakes
with Gus at your side, his great tail swinging,

but you will not reappear, tired and satisfied,
and grief's repeated particles suffuse the air —
like the dog yipping through the entire night,
or the cat stretching awake, then curling
as if to dream of her mother's milky nipples.

A raccoon dislodged a geranium from its pot.
Flowers, roots, and dirt lay upended
in the back garden where lilies begin
their daily excursions above stone walls
in the season of old roses. I pace beside weeds

and snowy peonies, staring at Mount Kearsarge
where you climbed wearing purple hiking boots.
"Hurry back. Be careful, climbing down."
Your peonies lean their vast heads westward
as if they might topple. Some topple.

After Three Years

You think that their
dying is the worst
thing that could happen.

Then they stay dead.

In a week or ten days
the snow and ice will melt
from Graveyard Road.

I'm coming! Don't move!

Kill the Day

When she died it was as if his car accelerated
off the pier's end and zoomed upward over death water
for a year without gaining or losing altitude,
then plunged to the bottom of the sea where his corpse
lay twisted in a honeycomb of steel, still dreaming
awake, as dead as she was but conscious still.
There is nothing so selfish as misery nor so boring,
and depression is devoted only to its own practice.
Mourning resembles melancholia precisely except
that melancholy adds self-loathing to stuporous sorrow

and turns away from the dead its exclusive attention.
Mania is melancholy reversed. Bereavement, loss,
and guilt provide excitement for conversion
to dysphoria, murderous rage, and unsleeping joy.
When he rose from the painted bed, he alternated or cycled
from dedicated hatred through gaiety and inflation
to the vacancy of breathing in-and-out, in-and-out.
He awakened daily to the prospect of nothingness
in the day's house that like all houses was mortuary.
He slept on the fornicating bed of the last breath.

He closed her eyes in the noon of her middle life;
he no longer cut and pruned for her admiration;
he worked for the praise of women and they died.
For months after her chest went still, he nightmared
that she had left him for another man. Everything

became its opposite and returned to itself.
As the second summer of her death approached him,
goldfinches flew at her feeder like daffodils
with wings and he could no longer tell her so.
Her absence could no longer be written to.

He emptied her shelves, dressers, and closets,
stacking rings and bracelets, pendants and necklaces.
He bundled sweaters and jeans, brassieres and blouses,
scarves and nightgowns and suits and summer dresses
and mailed them to Rosie's Place for indigent women.
For decades a man and a woman living together
learned each other for pleasure, giving and taking,
studying every other day predictable ecstasy
secure without secrecy or adventure, without romance,
without anxiety or jealousy, without content

except for the immaculate sexual content of sex.
The toad sat still for the toad's astounding moment,
but the day wasted whatever lived for the day
and the only useful desire obliterates desire.
Now the one day extended into multiple encounters
with loneliness that could not endure a visitor.
Machinery corroded in the barn no longer entered,
and no smoke rose from the two opposite chimneys.
It is naïve to complain over death and abandonment,
and the language of houses praised only itself.

Bone's Orchard bragged of breakfast and work, church
with neighbors on Sunday, gardening, the pond, and love
in the afternoon. The day ignored that it undertook
mere interruption on the trudge to fathomless loss.
"The days you work," said O'Keeffe, "are the best days."
Work without love is idle, idleness doing its job
for the velvet approbation of kings and presidents
without art's purpose to excite a lover's pleasure.
He turned into the ash heap damp in the Glenwood,
the burnt shape and constitution of wretchedness

in his ludicrous rage that things are as they are.
When she died, at first the outline of absence defined
a presence that disappeared. He wept for the body
he could no longer reach to touch in bed on waking.
He wept for her silver thimble. He wept when the dog
brought him a slipper that smelled of her still.
In another summer, her pheromones diminished.
The negative space of her body dwindled as she receded
deeper into the ground, smaller and fainter each day,
dried out, shrunken, separated from the news of the day.

When the coffee cup broke, when her yellow bathrobe
departed the bathroom door, when the address book
in her hand altered itself into scratchings-out,
he dreaded an adventure of self-hatred accomplished
by the finger or toe of an old man alone without

an onion to eat between slices of store-bought bread.
There was nothing to do, and nothing required doing.
Her vanishing constructed a blue synagogue
in a universe without solace or a task for doing.
He imagined that on shelves at his workroom's end

lay stacked two hundred and sixty-seven tiny
corpses, bodies of her body, porcelain mannequins.
In this dream or story he had neglected to bury them;
it was something still to do, something to be done.
In the second year, into the third and fourth years,
she died again and again, she died by receding
while he recited each day the stanzas of her dying:
He watched her chest go still; he closed her eyes.
Without birthdays, she remained her age at death.
The figurine broke that clutched its fists

as she did dying. In the pantry there were cans
and boxes and jars she bought in the supermarket
seven years ago. He walked through the vacancies,
burying her again. He had imagined an old man
alone in this white house, looking in the mirror.
Looking in the mirror now, he was old and alone.
He felt solitude's relief and intolerably lonely.
He envied whatever felt nothing: He envied oak
sills and the green hill rising and the boulder
by the side of the road and his dead love rotting

in her best white dress inside Vermont hardwood.
It was useful to set his name on her black granite,
but imminent or eventual cellular junction provided
the comfort of stone: to keep her safe beside him.
Visions of pleasure departed when she departed.
The condition of contentment or satisfaction
remains unattainable because of affect's agreement:
Whatever the measure of joy in the day's day,
no pleasure carries with it one part in ten million
of agony's vastation in loss and abandonment.

Therefore the condition of being alive is intolerable,
with no reason for endurance except that DNA
continues itself in order to continue itself.
Agreeing to love each other, they perfected a system:
Love is the exchange of a double narcissism,
agreement of twin surrender, the weapons laid-by,
the treaty enforced by habitual daily negotiation.
What would he do if he could do what he wanted?
The day prevented him from doing what he wanted.
Now he woke each morning wretched with morning's

regret that he woke. He woke looking forward
to a nap, to a cigarette, to supper, to port measured,
to sleep blessed sleep on the permanent painted bed
of death: Sleep, rage, kill the day, and die.
When she died, he died also. For the first year

his immediate grief confused him into feeling alive.
He endured the grief of a two-month love affair.
When women angry and free generously visited
the frenzy of his erotic grief, melancholia
became ecstasy, then sank under successful dirt.

Without prospect or purpose, who dared to love meat
that will putrefy? He rejoiced that he was meat.
How many times would he die in his own lifetime?
When TWA 800 blew out of the sky, his heart ascended
and exploded in gratitude, finding itself embodied
and broken as fragments scattering into water.
Then little green testicles dropped from the oaks
on New Canada Road again, another August of death,
and autumn McIntoshes rotted on the dwarf trees
already pecked by the loathsome birds of July.

Each day identified itself as a passage to elsewhere,
which was a passage to elsewhere and to elsewhere.
What did she look like now? Dried and slackening maybe.
Did the worms eat her? He supposed that they ate her.
Now he dreamed again of her thick and lavish hair,
of her lush body wetting and loosening beside him.
He remembered ordinary fucking that shone like the sun
in their household solar system, brighter than Jesus,
than poetry, than their orchard under the mountain —
the crossing place of bodies that regarded each other

with more devotion the more they approached her death
until they were singular, gazing speechless together
while she vanished into open eyes staring all night.
In the day's crush and tangle of melted nails,
collapsed foundation stones, and adze-trimmed beams,
the widower alone glimpsed the beekeeper's mask
in high summer as it approached the day they built,
now fallen apart with bark still on its beams,
nine layers of wallpaper over the dry laths —
always ending, no other ending, in dead eyes open.

The Revolution

I sort through left-behind
    Boxes that keep
    A muddled heap
Of women's work. I find
Wool squares she used to knit
While I sat opposite.

"Leftover life to kill,"
    Young Caitlin said
    With Dylan dead,
Yet lived with an ill will
Forty posthumous years
Of rage, fucking, and tears.

At seventy I taste
    In solitude
    Starvation's food,
As the land goes to waste
Where her death overthrew
A government of two.

Her Garden

I let her garden go.
let it go, let it go
How can I watch the hummingbird
Hover to sip
With its beak's tip
The purple bee balm — whirring as we heard
It years ago?

The weeds rise rank and thick
let it go, let it go
Where annuals grew and burdock grows,
Where standing she
At once could see
The peony, the lily, and the rose
Rise over brick

She'd laid in patterns. Moss
let it go, let it go
Turns the bricks green, softening them
By the gray rocks
Where hollyhocks
That lofted while she lived, stem by tall stem,
Dwindle in loss.

Pond Afternoons

When early July's
Arrival quieted the spring's black flies,
    We spent green afternoons
        Stretched on the moss
Beside dark Eagle Pond, and heard across
Its distances the calling of the loons.

    The days swam by,
Lazy with slow content and the hawk's cry.
    We lost ambition's rage,
        Forgot it all,
Forgot Jane Kenyon, forgot Donald Hall,
And sleepily half glanced at a bright page.

    Day after day
We crossed the flaking railroad tracks and lay
    In the slant August sun
        To nap and read
Beneath an oak, by the pond's pickerelweed.
Then acorns fell. These days were almost done.

Summer Kitchen

In June's high light she stood at the sink
    With a glass of wine,
And listened for the bobolink,
And crushed garlic in late sunshine.

I watched her cooking, from my chair.
    She pressed her lips
Together, reached for kitchenware,
And tasted sauce from her fingertips.

"It's ready now. Come on," she said.
    "You light the candle."
We ate, and talked, and went to bed,
And slept. It was a miracle.

Death Work

Wake when dog whimpers. Prick
Finger. Inject insulin.
    Glue teeth in.
   Smoke cigarette.
    Shudder and fret.
Feed old dog. Revise syllabic

On self-pity. Get *Boston Globe.*
Drink coffee. Eat bagel. Read
    At nervous speed.
   Smoke cigarette.
    Never forget
To measure oneself against Job.

Drag out afternoon.
Walk dog. Don't write.
    Turn off light.
   Smoke cigarette
    Watching sun set.
Wait for the fucking moon.

Nuke lasagna. Pace and curse.
For solitude's support
    Drink Taylor's port.
   Smoke cigarette.
    Sleep. Sweat.
Nightmare until dog whimpers.

The Wish

I keep her weary ghost inside me.
"Oh, let me go," I hear her crying.
"Deep in your dark you want to hide me
And so perpetuate my dying.
        I can't undo
        The grief that you
Weep by the stone where I am lying.
            Oh, let me go."

By work and women half distracted,
I endure the day and sleep at night
To watch her dying reenacted
When the faint dawn descends like twilight.
        How can I let
        This dream forget
Her white withdrawal from my sight,
            And let her go?

Her body while I watch grows smaller;
Her face recedes, her kiss is colder.
Watching her disappear, I call her
Again and again as I grow older
        While somewhere deep
        In the catch of sleep
I hear her cry, when I reach to hold her,
            "Oh, let me go!"

Ardor

After she died I screamed,
upsetting the depressed dog.
Now I no longer
address the wall
covered with photographs,
nor call her "you"
in a poem. She recedes
into the granite museum
of JANE KENYON 1947–1995.

Nursing her I felt alive
in the animal moment,
scenting the predator.
Her death was the worst thing
that could happen,
and caring for her was best.

I long for the absent
woman of different faces
who makes metaphors
and chops onion, drinking
a glass of Chardonnay,
oiling the wok, humming
to herself, maybe thinking
how to conclude a poem.
When I make love now,
something is awry.

Last autumn a woman said,
"I mistrust your ardor."

This winter in Florida
I loathed the old couples
my age who promenaded
in their slack flesh
holding hands. I gazed
at young women with outrage
and desire — unable to love
or to work, or to die.

Hours are slow and weeks
rapid in their vacancy.
Each day lapses as I recite
my complaints. Lust is grief
that has turned over in bed
to look the other way.

Conversation

Waking we sat with coffee
And smoked another cigarette
As quietly
Eros and affection met
In conversation's afterplay
On our first day.
Then late for the work you love, you drove away.

At dinner, just last night,
I looked at you, your bright green eyes
In candlelight.
We laughed, telling the hundred stories,
Caressed and kissed and went to bed.
"Shh, shh," you said,
"I want to put my legs around your head."

Sun

Both of us felt it: That day was an island,
strewn with rocks and lighthouses and lovers,
in the generous ocean. On the mainland,
people went about their business, eating
the *Times*, glancing through coffee and oatmeal,
as we walked the gangway into an original dream
of attentiveness, as if a day's pleasure
could concentrate us as much as suffering,
as if the seawall were a banquet without
surfeit, as if we could walk hand in hand
with no one nearby, as if silence and blue
wind became an Atlantic cove to float in,
and the air centered itself in small purple
butterflies flitting among the weed flowers.
In the darkening city we returned to,
our privacy completed the cafés of strangers.

Spring Glen Grammar School

        Sitting in the back seat
of a nineteen thirty-five Packard
        with running boards, I held
my great-uncle Luther's blotchy hand.
        He was nine for Appomattox
and remembered the soldier
        boys coming home from the war.
When I pressed the skin of his hand
        between thumb and forefinger,
the flesh turned white as Wonder Bread.
        It remained indented
for a few seconds and then rose up,
        turning pink, flush to the surface
of his veined hairless mottled
        hand. Then I pressed it again.
Luther would stay old forever.
        I would remain six, just
beginning first grade, learning to read.

        For weeks we learned
the alphabet — practicing it, reciting
        in unison singsong,
printing letters in block capitals
        on paper with wide blue
lines, responding out loud to flash cards.
        Then she said: "Tomorrow
you'll learn to read."

                    Miss Stephanie Ford
           wrote on the blackboard
in large square letters: T H A T. "That,"
           she said, gesticulating
with her wooden pointer, "is 'that.'"

           Each year began
in September with the new room and a new
           teacher: I started with
Stephanie Ford, then Miss Flint, Miss Gold,
           Miss Sudel whom I loved,
Miss Stroker, Miss Fehm, Miss Pikosky . . .
           I was announcer
at assemblies. I was elected class
           president not because
I was popular but because I
           was polite to grown-ups, spoke
distinctly, held my hands straight down
           at my sides, and kept
my shirt tucked in: I was presidential.

           Eight years in this
rectangular brick of the nineteen thirties:
           If I survive to be eighty,
this box will contain the tithe
           of a long life.

In the glass case, terra is miniature:
tiny snails and mosses,
wooden houses with sidewalks, small trees,
and Spring Glen Grammar School.
See, pupils gather around a boy
in black knickers
who shoots an agate, kneeling in the circle.

1943

They toughened us for war. In the high school auditorium
Ed Monahan knocked out Dominick Esposito in the first round

of the heavyweight finals, and ten months later Dom died
in the third wave at Tarawa. Every morning of the war

our Brock-Hall Dairy delivered milk from horse-drawn wagons
to wooden back porches in southern Connecticut. In winter,

frozen cream lifted the cardboard lids of glass bottles,
grade A or grade B, while Marines bled to death in the surf,

or the right engine faltered into Channel silt, or troops marched
— what could we do? — with frostbitten feet as white as milk.

The Things

When I walk in my house I see pictures,
bought long ago, framed and hanging
— de Kooning, Arp, Laurencin, Henry Moore —
that I've cherished and stared at for years,
yet my eyes keep returning to the masters
of the trivial — a white stone perfectly round,
tiny lead models of baseball players, a cowbell,
a broken great-grandmother's rocker,
a dead dog's toy — valueless, unforgettable
detritus that my children will throw away
as I did my mother's souvenirs of trips
with my dead father, Kodaks of kittens,
and bundles of cards from her mother Kate.

Tennis Ball

I parked by the grave in September, under oaks and birches,
and said hello again, and went walking with Gussie

past markers, roses, and the grave with plastic chickens.
(Somebody loved somebody who loved chickens.)

Gus stopped and stared: A woman's long bare legs
stretched up at the edge of the graveyard, a man's body

heaving between them. Gus considered checking them out,
so I clicked my fingers, as softly as I could, to distract him,

and became the unintended source of *coitus interruptus.*
Walking to the car, I peeked. She was restarting him, her

head riding up and down. It was a fine day, leaves red,
Gus healthy and gay, refusing to give up his tennis ball.

Affirmation

To grow old is to lose everything.
Aging, everybody knows it.
Even when we are young,
we glimpse it sometimes, and nod our heads
when a grandfather dies.
Then we row for years on the midsummer
pond, ignorant and content. But a marriage,
that began without harm, scatters
into debris on the shore,
and a friend from school drops
cold on a rocky strand.
If a new love carries us
past middle age, our wife will die
at her strongest and most beautiful.
New women come and go. All go.
The pretty lover who announces
that she is temporary
is temporary. The bold woman,
middle-aged against our old age,
sinks under an anxiety she cannot withstand.
Another friend of decades estranges himself
in words that pollute thirty years.
Let us stifle under mud at the pond's edge
and affirm that it is fitting
and delicious to lose everything.

The Coffee Cup

The newspaper, the coffee cup, the dog's
impatience for his morning walk.
These fibers bind the ordinary mystery.
After the marriage of lovers
the children came, and the schoolbus
that stopped to pick up the children,

and the expected death of the retired
mailman Anthony "Cat" Middleton
who drove the schoolbus for a whole
schoolyear, a persistence enduring
forever in the soul of Marilyn
who was six years old that year.

We dug a hole for him. When his widow
Florence sold the Cape and moved to town
to live near her daughter, the Mayflower
van was substantial and unearthly.
Neither lymphoma nor a brown-and-white
cardigan twenty years old

made an exception, not elbows nor
Chevrolets nor hills cutting blue
shapes on blue sky, not Maple Street
nor Main, not a pink-striped canopy
over an ice cream store, not grass.
It was ordinary that on the day

of Cat's funeral the schoolbus arrived
driven by a woman called Mrs. Ek,
freckled and thin, wearing a white
bandana and overalls, with one
eye blue and the other gray. Everything
is strange; nothing is strange:

yarn, the moon, gray hair in a bun,
New Hampshire, putting on socks.

Hawk's Crag

You climb Hawk's Crag, a cellphone in your baggy shorts,
and gaze into the leafing trees and famous blue water.
You telephone, in love with the skin of the world. I hear you
puff as you start to climb down, still talking, switching
your phone from hand to hand as the holds require.

You sing showtunes sitting above me, clicking your fingers,
swaying your shadowy torso. We flow into each other
in a sensuous dazzle as global and attendant as suffering
until a gradual gathering surges like water over the dam
and together we soar level across the durable lake.

But how can one flesh and consciousness adhere to another,
when we know that every adherence ends in separation?
I long for your return, your face lit by a candle, your smile
private as a kore's under an inconstant flame — as I stare
into the flat and black of water, knowing that we will drown.

Black Olives

"Dead people don't like black olives,"
I told my partners in eighth grade
dancing class, who never listened
as we foxtrotted, one-*two*, one-*two*.

The dead people I often consulted
nodded their skulls in unison
while I flung my black velvet cape
over my shoulders and glowered
from deep-set, burning eyes,
walking the city streets, alone at fifteen,
crazy for cheerleaders and poems.

At Hamden High football games, girls
in short pleated skirts
pranced and kicked, and I longed
for their memorable thighs.
They were *friendly* — poets were mascots —
but never listened when I told them
that dead people didn't like black olives.

Instead the poet, wearing his cape,
continued to prowl in solitude
intoning inscrutable stanzas
while halfbacks and tackles
made out, Friday nights after football,
on sofas in knotty-pine rec rooms
with magnanimous cheerleaders.

Decades later, after the dead
have stopped their blathering
about olives, obese halfbacks wheeze
upstairs to sleep beside cheerleaders
waiting for hip replacements,
while a lascivious, doddering poet,
his burning eyes deep-set
in wrinkles, cavorts with their daughters.

The Master

Where the poet stops, the poem
begins. The poem asks only
that the poet get out of the way.

The poem empties itself
in order to fill itself up.

The poem is nearest the poet
when the poet laments
that it has vanished forever.

When the poet disappears
the poem becomes visible.

What may the poem choose,
best for the poet?
It will choose that the poet
not choose for himself.

Meatloaf

1. Twenty-five years ago, Kurt Schwitters,
I tried to instruct you in baseball
but kept getting distracted, gluing
bits and pieces of world history
alongside personal anecdote
instead of explicating baseball's
habits. I was K.C. (for Casey)
in stanzas of nine times nine times nine.
Last year the Sox were ahead by twelve

2. in May, by four in August — collapsed
as usual — then won the Series.
Jane Kenyon, who loved baseball, enjoyed
the game on TV but fell asleep
by the fifth inning. She died twelve years
ago, and thus would be sixty now,
watching baseball as her hair turned white.
I see her tending her hollyhocks,
gazing west at Eagle Pond, walking

3. to the porch favoring her right knee.
I live alone with baseball each night
but without poems. One of my friends
called "Baseball" *almost* poetry. No
more vowels carrying images
leap suddenly from my excited
unwitting mind and purple Bic pen.

As he aged, Auden said that methods
of dry farming may also grow crops.

4. When Jane died I had constant nightmares
that she left me for somebody else.
I bought condoms, looking for affairs,
as distracting as Red Sox baseball
and even more subject to failure.
There was love, there was comfort; always
something was wrong, or went wrong later
— her adultery, my neediness —
until after years I found Linda.

5. When I was named Poet Laureate,
the kids of Danbury School painted
baseballs on a kitchen chair for me,
with two lines from "Casey at the Bat."
In fall I lost sixty pounds, and lost
poetry. I studied only *Law
and Order*. My son took from my house
the eight-sided Mossberg .22
my father gave me when I was twelve.

6. Buy two pounds of cheap fat hamburger
so the meatloaf will be sweet, chop up
a big onion, add leaves of basil,
Tabasco, newspaper ads, soy sauce,

quail eggs, driftwood, tomato ketchup,
and library paste. Bake for ten hours
at thirty-five degrees. When pitchers
hit the batter's head, Kurt, it is called
a beanball. The batter takes first base.

7. After snowdrifts melted in April,
I gained pounds back, and with Linda flew
to Paris, eating all day: croissants
warm, crisp, and buttery, then baguettes
Camembert, at last boeuf bourguignon
with bottles of red wine. Afternoons
we spent in the Luxembourg Gardens
or in museums: the Marmottan!
the Pompidou! the Orangerie!

8. the Musée de la Vie Romantique!
the Louvre! the d'Orsay! the Jeu de
Paume! the Musée Maillol! the Petit
Palais! When the great Ted Williams died,
his son detached his head and froze it
in a Scottsdale depository.
In summer, enduring my dotage,
I try making this waterless farm,
"Meatloaf," with many ingredients.

9. In August Linda climbs Mount Kearsarge,
where I last clambered in middle age,
while I sit in my idle body
in the car, in the cool parking lot,
revising these lines for Kurt Schwitters,
counting nine syllables on fingers
discolored by old age and felt pens,
my stanzas like ballplayers sent down
to Triple-A, too slow for the bigs.

POSTSCRIPTUM

When I was twelve I wrote my first poem, and by fourteen I decided that's what I'd do my whole life. I don't regret it. After spending decades trying to practice a great art, now I concentrate on making a selection from my poems — for you to decide how much or how little I've done. It's strange yet a pleasure to pick and choose, going through the up-and-down story of a life. My son my executioner is born; I endure my father's early death; I marry Jane Kenyon and we move to New Hampshire; Jane thrives as we write poems together; Jane dies; I survive and turn old.

As I read my poems in chronological order, I am aware of changing sounds and shapes. I move from rhymed stanzas to varieties of free verse, and later — out of love for Thomas Hardy's poems — go back to meter again. Not every poet's manner alters so much as mine does. Most of my best contemporaries repeat a characteristic shape and style. So have most sculptors and painters, and we do not mistake Cézanne for van Gogh. But Henry Moore's shelter drawings do not resemble his reclining figures which do not resemble his black-faced sheep. I chose among my poems partly to acknowledge changes in style.

The last time I did a selection it was huge. This time I am more selective, using a third as many poems. Less is more. I choose the poems I judge best. Some, from the day I wrote them, have remained uppermost in my mind. I remember the preferences of others, often showing me qualities that I had not consciously intended.

Reading my things aloud a thousand times I have become aware of language that works and language that has dead spots. Now that I'll make no more poems, I want to collect a concise gathering of my life's work.

Choosing my poems, willy-nilly I emphasize my obsessions. I've told the story before, how a grumpy stranger asked me, "What do you write about, anyway?" I blurted out, "Love, death, and New Hampshire." It's true. Love, death, and love's death — in early poems maybe love for death? — and always Eagle Pond Farm. When Jane and I moved here from Ann Arbor, where I taught, we were blissful in our new landscape and in my ancestral family place. We loved living alone in the country, with each other and with poetry, at the farm where I spent old summers haying with my grandfather. At first, Jane's poems considered how she might fit in, adapting to somebody else's century-old place. She *fit*. We wrote about where we lived. We wrote about each other.

After Jane died of leukemia at forty-seven — on our painted bed in our bedroom — for five years I wrote about nothing but her death.

Most of my life, I have worked on poems each morning, fiddling with everything. I have crossed out a word and substituted another; the next day I have often returned to the first word, or found yet another. Or I have broken a line at a new place. Always when I finished a poem, I showed it to friends who told me if it was terrible, or at least suggested improvements. I did the same for them.

Sometimes I revised a poem long after I thought I had finished it. In 1955, on Christmas Eve in a Connecticut neighborhood called Whitneyville, we buried my fifty-two-year-old father. The next month I began "Christmas Eve in Whitneyville," fourteen pentameter quatrains rhymed *abab*. Near its end I wrote that everybody fell asleep, and at first the somnolence was transcontinental: "Across America, when midnight comes . . ." I published it in a magazine and a book. Thirteen years later, in a selected poems, I altered my Whitmanic wingspan. "Across America" expanded into "All over Whitneyville . . ."

After we married, Jane and I worked together over each other's poems. We did not look at early drafts — it's a bad habit; wait until the poem solidifies — but when the poems felt done, each of us used the other as first reader. One day I would say, "I left some stuff on your footstool," or Jane would tell me, "Perkins, there are some things on your desk." ("Perkins" was me.) If I repeated a word — a twist acquired from Yeats — Jane crossed it out. Whenever she used verbal auxiliaries I removed them, and "it was raining" became "it rained." Jane kept her lines clear of dead metaphor, knowing my crankiness on the subject. She exulted when she found one in my drafts: "Perkins! Here's a dead metaphor!"

These encounters were essential but not always easy. Sometimes we turned polite with each other: "Oh, really! I thought that was the best part . . . heh, heh." Jane told others — people questioned us about how we worked — that I approached her holding a sheaf of her poems saying, "These are going to be good!" And she would reply, "Going to be, eh?" As she climbed back to her study — she told everyone —"I thought that Perkins just didn't get it! Then I'd do everything he said!"

Neither of us did everything the other said. We helped each other vastly. She saved me from a thousand gaffes, cut my wordiness and straightened out my syntax. She seldom told me that anything was good. Sometimes she'd say, "This is almost done," or "You've brought this a long way, Perkins." I asked, "But is it any *good?*" I pined for her praise. It was essential that we never go easy on each other. I remember one evening in 1992 when we sat in the living room as she read through the manuscript of my *Museum of Clear Ideas,* which was unlike anything I had done before. I watched her dark face as she turned the pages. Finally she looked over at me and tears started from her eyes. "Perkins, I don't *like* it!" Tears came to my eyes too, and I said, "That's okay. That's okay."

The better Jane wrote, the more honors came her way, the more I took care not to sound like her. After she died I no longer worried about it. I wrote for two. My first mourning poem, "Weeds and Peonies," used words that resounded in her work.

People have long assumed that poets flourish when they are young, but for most poets their best work comes in middle life. Wallace Stevens said, "Some of one's early things give one the creeps." A friend insists that no one should publish a poem written after eighty. I hope I wrote good things, young and old, but my best work came in my early sixties. Over the years I felt my poems gradually diminish. I lost my powers as everyone does. It was frustrating at first, but finally I accepted the inevitable. How could I complain, after seventy years of ambition and pleasure? Happily I am able to write prose. *Essays After Eighty* came out in 2014.

9 781328 745606